CW00977702

This is a Parragon Book.

© Parragon 1997

Parragon
13-17 Avonbridge Trading Estate
Atlantic Road, Avonmouth
Bristol, BS11 9QD

Produced by The Templar Company plc,
Pippbrook Mill, London Road, Dorking,
Surrey RH4 1JE

Written by Robert Snedden
Illustrated by Tony Gibbons
Series Designer Mark Summersby

Printed and bound in the UK

ISBN 0 7525 1684 1

FACTFINDERS

WORLD WAR II
COMBAT
AIRCRAFT

P

· PARRAGON ·

Titles in this Series Include:

Astronomy

Card Games

Clans & Tartans

Fastest Cars

Flags of the World

Freshwater Fish

Garden Birds

Handguns & Small Arms

Historic Britain

Human Body

Insects

Inventions

Modern Combat Aircraft

Natural Disasters

Pond Life

Rocks & Fossils

Wild Flowers

World War II Combat Aircraft

CONTENTS

Introduction 8

France

Dewoitine D520 12

Germany

Dornier Do335 Pfeil 14

Focke-Wulf Fw 190. 16

Heinkel He162
Salamander 18

Heinkel He219 Uhu 20

Junkers Ju 87. 22

Messerschmitt Bf109. . . . 24

Messerschmitt Bf110. . . . 26

Messerschmitt Me163
Komet 28

Messerschmitt Me262 . . . 30

Great Britain

Bristol Type 156
Beaufighter 32

De Havilland 98
Mosquito 34

Fairey Firefly. 36

Gloster G-41 Meteor . . . 38

Hawker Hurricane 40

Hawker Typhoon 42

Hawker Tempest. 44

Supermarine Spitfire. . . . 46

Westland Whirlwind 48

Italy

Macchi C.202. 50

Reggiáne Re 2000. 52

Japan

Kawanishi N1K2-J 54

Kawasaki Ki-61 56

Mitsubishi A6M
Zero-Sen 58

Nakajima Ki-43
Hayabusa. 60

Nakajima Ki-84 Hayate . 62

Soviet Union

Ilyushin Il-2 Stormovik . . 64

Mikoyan-Gurevich
MiG-3 66

Polikarpov I-16 68

Yakovlev Yak-1 70

United States

Curtiss P-40 Hawk 72

Grumman F4F Wildcat. . . 74

Grumman F6F Hellcat . . 76

Lockheed P-38
Lightning. 78

NA P-51 Mustang 80

Northrop P-61
Black Widow. 82

Republic P-47
Thunderbolt 84

Vought V-166 Corsair . . . 86

Air Power in
World War II. 88

Anatomy of a
Fighter Plane. 92

INTRODUCTION

One of the guiding principles behind the development of the British and United States air forces in the build-up to World War II was the belief that bombers could win the war. The Germans, on the other hand, built up a force of light bombers and ground attack fighters that would work with their ground troops.

The British soon learned the necessity of producing fighter aircraft, both to provide protection from the German bombers that swarmed over Britain after the fall of France, and also to provide some sort of escort cover for their bomber fleets, which suffered terrible losses as they attempted to carry the war to Germany. In the Battle of Britain in the summer of 1940, RAF forces of scarcely more than 600 aircraft faced over 2,700 Luftwaffe planes. Yet within two years the Germans hardly dared to cross into British skies at all.

Throughout the war, fighter aircraft development proved to be a survival of the fittest with the designers and engineers of, for example, the Hawker Hurricane and Supermarine Spitfire on the British side and the Messerschmitt Bf109 and FockeWulf Fw190 on the German side, struggling to achieve and maintain superiority in the air over their rivals.

On the Pacific Front, the Japanese convincingly demonstrated the effectiveness of airpower with the surprise attack by carrier-based aircraft on the American fleet at Pearl Harbor, on 7 December, 1941, when they succeeded in damaging 8 battleships, 10 warships, and 349 aircraft, and killed or wounded 3,581 troops.

Aircraft could inflict damaging losses on enemy forces through sheer weight of numbers. The Soviet Ilyushin Il-2 Stormovik was a prime example. More than 40,000 of this frankly mediocre, armoured ground-attack fighter were produced and they swarmed over the German ground forces on the Eastern Front, attacking troops, tanks and supply convoys.

More aircraft were built during the Second World War than at any time since. Great steps were being made in technical development, including the first appearance of jet aircraft. But of course, it wasn't all down to the technology. Of vital importance too was the courage, daring and sheer flying skills of the pilots who flew these great aircraft. Some Luftwaffe pilots had flown over a thousand combat missions by the end of the war, in vain trying to hold back the tide of Allied airmen breaking over their country. The sacrifices made by brave men on all sides of the conflict should not be forgotten.

DEWOITINE D520

Type:	single-seat fighter
Engines:	910hp Hispano-Suiza 12Y-45, liquid cooled
Wingspan:	10.2m (33ft 6in)
Length:	8.75m (28ft 8in)
Height:	3.4m (11ft 3in)
Weight:	2100kg (4630lb) empty, 2800kg (6170lb) loaded
Maximum speed:	530km/h (329mph)
Service ceiling:	11,000m (36,090 ft)
Maximum range:	1240km (777 miles)
Armament:	one 20mm Hispano-Suiza cannon firing through propeller, four 7.5mm MAC 1934 machine-guns in wings
First flight:	27 November 1938

The Dewoitine D520 was only just made ready in time to see active service against the Luftwaffe. The first prototype was wrecked on its first flight on 27 November 1938, when the test pilot forgot to let down the landing gear. Although production was three months behind schedule in 1939, such was the impetus given by the outbreak of war that the factories went into overdrive. By May 1940 a hundred had been delivered and by the following month aircraft were coming off the production line at the rate of ten a day. In the short time before the fall of France on 22 June the Dewoitine squadrons were credited with 147 kills for the loss of just 85 fighters. Production of the D520 was recommenced by the Vichy government, some seeing service with the Luftwaffe.

DORNIER DO335 PFEIL

Type:	single-seat fighter (A-1); two-seat night fighter (A-6)
Engines:	two 1900hp Daimler-Benz
Wingspan:	13.8m (45ft 4in)
Length:	13.87m (45ft 6in)
Height:	4m (16ft 4in)
Weight:	A-1: 7400kg (16,341lb), A-6: 7700kg (16,975lb) empty, both 11,700kg (25,800lb) loaded
Maximum speed:	A-1: (765km/h/477mph with emergency boost)
Service ceiling:	A-1: 11,410 metres (37,400ft)
Maximum range:	2050km (1280 miles); 3750km (2330 miles) with drop tank
Armament:	A-1: one 30mm MK103 cannon, two 15mm MG151/15 above nose; centreline rack for 500kg (1100lb) bomb
First flight:	autumn 1943

The Do335 was easily distinguished by its rear-mounted second 'pusher' propeller. Although capable of very high speeds, the 335 was liable to buck uncomfortably when it was flown fast. It was the first plane to be produced with an ejection seat (baling out in the usual fashion could have unpleasant consequences for an airman caught by the rear propeller). Only around 20 of these unusual planes were actually delivered to combat units before VE-Day, although more than four times that number were to come off the production line. At the end of the war, there were plans afoot to produce the Do635 reconnaissance plane, which would link two 335 fuselages with a new centre section and so weigh three times as much. 'Pfeil' means arrow.

FOCKE-WULF Fw190

Type:	single-seat fighter bomber
Engines:	1700hp BMW 801Dg 18-cylinder radial (2100hp with emergency boost)
Wingspan:	10.49m (34ft 5in)
Length:	8.84m (29ft)
Height:	3.96m (13ft)
Weight:	3200kg (7055lb) empty, 4900kg (10,800lb) loaded
Maximum speed:	653km/h (408mph) with boost
Service ceiling:	11,410m (37,400ft)
Maximum range:	900km (560 miles)
Armament:	two 13mm MG 131 positioned above engine, two 20mm MG 1512/20 in wing roots, two MG 151/20s or 30mm MK 108s in outer wings, centreline rack for one 500kg (1100lb) bomb
First flight:	1 June 1939

The Focke-Wulf Fw190 came in a number of combat variants and was produced in a number of different versions in factories scattered across Germany. Some were equipped with tank-destroying Panzerblitz rockets and used as close-support attack aircraft, some were equipped with torpedoes for assaults on shipping and others were specially armoured to allow them to ram Allied heavy bombers in mid-air. When the Fw 190 first appeared in combat over Europe in early 1941 it totally out-performed the RAF's Spitfire V and was faster and better armed than any Allied aircraft then available. In total over 20,000 Fw 190s were delivered before the end of the war and throughout the conflict it continued to be one of the most formidable planes in the air.

HEINKEL HE162 SALAMANDER

Type:	single-seat interceptor
Engines:	one BMW 003E-1 or E-2 Orkan single shaft turbojet
Wingspan:	7.2m (23ft 8in)
Length:	9m (29ft 8in)
Height:	2.6m (6ft 6in)
Weight:	2180kg (4796lb) empty, 2695kg (5940lb) loaded
Maximum speed:	784km/h (490mph) at sea level; 835km/h (522mph) at 6000m (19,700ft)
Service ceiling:	12,040m (39,500ft)
Maximum range:	695km (434 miles) at full throttle
Armament:	two 30mm Rheinmetall MK 108 cannon with 50 rounds each, later two 20mm Mauser MG 151/20 with 120 rounds each
First flight:	6 December 1944

The futuristic Heinkel He162 Salamander was also known as the Volksjäger, the People's Fighter. Its progress from drawing board at the end of October 1944 to delivery in January 1945 was achieved with remarkable speed, especially since at the time Germany was being bombed daily by Allied heavy bombers and its industries and supply lines were in ruins. Armies of workers were pressed into service to get the plane ready and members of the Hitler Youth, most of the Luftwaffe's experienced aircrew having been killed, were hastily trained to fly it. The prototype, a tiny wooden plane with its powerful turbojet perched on top behind the cockpit, flew just over a month after the designs were completed. By VE-Day, 8 May 1945, 300 Salamanders had been built.

HEINKEL HE219 UHU

Type:	two-seat night fighter
Engines:	two 1900hp Daimler-Benz DB 603G, liquid-cooled inverted-vee 12
Wingspan:	18.5m (60ft 8in)
Length:	15.54m (51ft) with aerials
Height:	4.1m (13ft 5in)
Weight:	11,200kg (24,692lb) empty, 15,200kg (33,730lb) loaded
Maximum speed:	670km/h (416mph)
Service ceiling:	12,700m (41,660ft)
Maximum range:	2000km (1243 miles)
Armament:	two 30mm MK 108s in the wing roots, two 30mm MK 108s and two MG 150/20s in the belly tray, two 30mm MK 108s in the upward-firing Schräge Musik (Jazz Music) installation for destroying bombers from below
First flight:	15 November 1942

The Heinkel He219 Uhu was originally conceived as a high-speed multi-role fighter, bomber and torpedo carrier, but the emphasis was switched to night-fighting when RAF raids grew more persistent towards the end of 1941. The early prototypes, fast and highly manoeuvrable, met with an enthusiastic response from the Luftwaffe and several hundred were ordered, although in the end less than 300 aircraft were actually produced. The first six missions undertaken by the He219s resulted in the destruction of 20 RAF bombers, among them a number of the previously practically indestructible Mosquitoes. More than 15 versions of the He219 were produced in the course of the war, differing in the type of armament carried. Uhu means owl.

JUNKERS JU87

Type:	two-seat ground attack and dive bomber (statistics are for Ju87D-1)
Engines:	1300hp Junker Jumo 211J
Wingspan:	13.8m (45ft 3in)
Length:	11.1m (36ft 5in)
Height:	3.9m (12ft 9in)
Weight:	2750kg (6080lb) empty, 5720kg (12,600lb) loaded
Maximum speed:	408km/h (255mph)
Service ceiling:	7320m (24,000ft)
Maximum range:	1000km (620 miles) carrying maximun load
Armament:	two 7.92mm Rheinmetall-Borsig MG 17 machine-guns in wings, two manually-aimed 7.92mm MG 81s in rear cockpit, one centre-mounted 1800kg (3968lb) bomb
First flight:	late 1935 (first D-1 in 1940)

The Junkers Ju87 Stuka was one of the most feared ground-attack aircraft of the early years of the Second World War, as it plunged down on enemy troops and convoys, siren wailing, to bomb and strafe. The Stuka was fitted with a device that would pull it up from its dive automatically, because experience had shown that pilots could lose consciousness. In the first campaigns of the war, in Poland and the Low Countries, the Ju87 was used to great effect against the defending forces. However, it proved to be no match for the Hurricanes and Spitfires of the RAF and so many were lost in the Battle of Britain that it was withdrawn from that theatre. In the latter part of the war it was employed on the Russian Front, specially equipped for attacks on armoured vehicles.

MESSERSCHMITT BF109

Type:	single-seat fighter (statistics are for E series)
Engines:	1100hp Daimler-Benz DB 601A, 1200hp DB 601N or 1300hp DB 601E
Wingspan:	9.87m (32ft 4in)
Length:	8.64m (28ft 4in)
Height:	2.28m (7ft 5in)
Weight:	1900kg (4189lb) empty, 2505kg (5523lb) loaded
Maximum speed:	560-570km/h (348-354mph)
Service ceiling:	10,500m (34,450ft)
Maximum range:	700km (438 miles)
Armament:	two 7.92mm Rheinmetall-Borsig MG 17s above engine, 20mm MG FF firing through propeller, two MG FFs in wings
First flight:	January 1939

The Messerschmitt Bf109 has been called one of the greatest combat aircraft ever flown. Early versions saw combat service in the Spanish Civil War, which began in 1936. The Bf109 was small and fast, with excellent acceleration and a good rate of climb; it was also cheap to produce and when Germany invaded Poland in 1939 the Bf109E was the Luftwaffe's most important fighter. With the exception of the Spitfire, no Allied aircraft could pose a serious threat to it. From 1943 the Bf109G was the dominant version. Although heavily armed, it wasn't as good an aircraft as the earlier E model and was much more demanding to fly. After the war, production of Bf109s continued in Czechoslovakia and in Spain. The last one left the factory in 1956.

MESSERSCHMITT Bf110

Type:	two-seat day/night fighter
Engines:	two 1100hp Daimler-Benz DB601A; later 1200hp DB601N; 1475hp DB605B
Wingspan:	16.25m (53ft 5in)
Length:	12.1m (39ft 8in)
Height:	3.5m (11ft 6in)
Weight:	4500kg (9920lb) empty, 7000kg (15,430lb) loaded
Maximum speed:	562km/h (349mph)
Service ceiling:	10,000m (32,800ft)
Maximum range:	850km (528 miles)
Armament:	20mm Oerlikon MG FF cannon, four 7.92mm Rheinmetall-Borsig MG17s in nose, one 7.92mm MG15 in rear cock pit, centre-rack for four 250kg (551lb) bombs, two 20mm MG151 in Schräge Musik installation on night fighters.
First flight:	12 May 1936 (Bf110V1 prototype)

The Messerschmitt BF110 was conceived as a long-range fighter escort, accompanying bomber fleets on raids deep inside enemy territory. The prototypes were clumsy and lacked manoeuvrability but had an impressive turn of speed. By 1939 and the invasion of Poland, the Luftwaffe had almost 200 Bf110 fighters and they acquitted themselves well, dealing easily with any opposition they encountered from Polish aircraft. As the German armies advanced through Western Europe, the Bf110s continued to demolish the opposing forces. It was only when they took on the Spitfires and Hurricanes of the RAF in the Battle of Britain that their weaknesses were exposed and they were shot down in great numbers. Later in the war a new night-fighter version saw service.

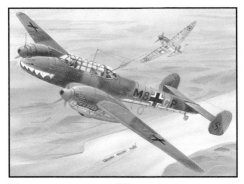

MESSERSCHMITT ME163 KOMET

Type:	single-seat interceptor
Engines:	one 1700kg (3750lb) thrust Walter HWK 509A-2 rocket, burning hydrogen peroxide and hydrazine/methanol
Wingspan:	9.3m (30ft 7in)
Length:	5.69m (18ft 8in)
Height:	2.74m (9ft)
Weight:	1905kg (4191lb) empty, 4110kg (9042lb) loaded
Maximum speed:	960km/h (596mph)
Service ceiling:	16,500m (54,000ft) (initial climb rate 5000m/16,400ft per minute)
Maximum range:	100km (62 miles) (maximum flight time around 8 minutes)
Armament:	two 60-round 30mm MK 108 cannon mounted in wing roots
First flight:	first powered flight August 1941

The Messerschmitt Me163 Komet was one of the most remarkable aircraft to see service in the Second World War. The chemical propellants used combined violently in the combustion chamber of the aircraft to provide thrust. The volatile nature of the propellants made the Komet dangerous to be near on the ground. The pilots were additionally endangered by its lack of landing gear. It landed instead on a skid and sometimes the force of the impact resulted in the explosive combination of any propellants left in the tanks. Most of the 370 Me 163s to see service were lost through accidents. Despite these flaws, the Komet was thought to have the best flying characteristics of any aircraft flown by the Luftwaffe and they caused considerable losses among Allied bombers.

MESSERSCHMITT ME262

Type: single-seat fighter-bomber, two-seat night-fighter

Engines: two 900kg (1980lb) thrust Junkers Jumo 004B turbojets

Wingspan: 12.5m (41ft)

Length: 10.6m (34ft 10in)

Height: 3.8m (12ft 7in)

Weight: single-seat 4000kg (8820lb) empty, 7045kg (15,500lb) loaded, two-seat 4400kg (9700lb)/ 6400kg (14,110lb)

Maximum speed: 860km/h (540mph) (single-seat fighter)

Service ceiling: 11,500m (37,565ft)

Maximum range: around 1050km (650 miles)

Armament: fighter: four 30mm MK 108 cannon in nose, later 24 R4/M 50mm rockets. night fighter: two MK 108s in Schräge Musik installation.

First flight: 18 July 1942 using turbojets

The Messerschmitt Me262 was faster and more heavily armed than any fighter the Allies could put up against it. Messerschmitt began working on a jet fighter design in 1938 and the first aircraft came off the production line in July 1944. In all, over 1400 Me262s were delivered before the end of the war. It was a devastating weapon that could have restored air supremacy over Germany to the Luftwaffe, were it not for Hitler's insistence that it be used for bombing raids. The night-fighter and stand-off attack versions also caused great damage to Allied bombing missions. The Allies had no effective defence against the Me 262, however its Junkers Jumo 004 engines proved to be unreliable and many aircraft were lost when their engines failed.

BRISTOL TYPE 156 BEAUFIGHTER

Type:	(Mark X) two-seat torpedo strike fighter (others night fighters)
Engines:	two 1770hp Bristol Hercules XVII
Wingspan:	17.63m (57ft 10in)
Length:	12.6m (41ft 8in)
Height:	4.84m (15ft 10in)
Weight:	7100kg (15,600lb) empty, 11,530kg (25,400lb) loaded
Maximum speed:	528km/h (330mph)
Service ceiling:	9144m (30,000ft)
Maximum range:	2478km (1540 miles)
Armamament:	four 20mm Hispano cannon on under side of fuselage, 0.303in Vickers K aimed by observer, six 0.303in Brownings, four in right wing, two in left, 728kg (1605lb) torpedo, racks for 8 rockets or two 454kg (1000lb) bombs
First flight:	17 July 1939 (Type 156 prototype)

The Type 156 Beaufighter was designed to fill a number of gaps in the RAF's capabilities in the years immediately prior to the Second World War. By incorporating wings, tail, landing gear and other systems from the existing Bristol Beaufort, designer Leslie Frise came up with an aircraft that could be produced quickly. The Beaufighter proved to be a fine combat aeroplane, formidably armed and highly manoeuvrable, it was particularly effective as a night fighter going against German bombers during the Blitz. A number of variants were produced and the Beaufighter served tellingly on all fronts during the war. The Japanese called it the 'whispering death' because its engines were so quiet. In total, almost 6000 were built, most in England and over 300 in Australia.

DE HAVILLAND 98 MOSQUITO

Type:	principally a high-speed day bomber, (statistics are for Mark VI)
Engines:	two 1230hp Rolls-Royce Merlin 21, later 1635hp Merlin 25
Wingspan:	16.5m (54ft 2in)
Length:	12.34m (40ft 6in)
Height:	4.7m (15ft 4in)
Weight:	6400kg (14,100lb) empty, 10,200kg (22,500lb) loaded
Maximum speed:	612km/h (380mph)
Service ceiling:	10,520m (34,500ft)
Maximum range:	around 2990km (1860 miles)
Armament:	four 20mm Hispano cannon, four 0.303 Brownings in nose, two 113kg (250lb) bombs in bay, plus two bombs, depth charges, or eight rockets, on wing racks
First flight:	25 November 1940 (prototype)

The basic design of the De Havilland Mosquito proved so successful that it gave rise to over twenty variants, with almost 8000 aircraft being built in Britain, Canada and Australia. However, the Air Ministry were initially reluctant to give the go ahead to the planned high-speed day bomber made largely of wood that was proposed in 1938 and development did not get properly underway until 1940. The first version was used for reconnaissance missions and later marks were employed as night fighters, unarmed bombers and fighter-bombers. There was even a Royal Navy Sea Mosquito with folding wings. In 1941, the Mosquito was the fastest plane in the sky. The Mark VI fighter-bomber was produced in greater numbers than any other variant, with over 2500 coming into service.

FAIREY FIREFLY

Type:	two-seat naval fighter (statistics are for the Mark I)
Engines:	one 1730hp Rolls-Royce Griffon IIB liquid-cooled, later 1990hp Griffon XII
Wingspan:	13.55m (44ft 6in)
Length:	11.4m (37ft 7in)
Height:	4.15m (13ft 7in)
Weight:	4422kg (9750lb) empty, 6359kg (14,020lb) loaded
Maximum speed:	509km/h (316mph)
Service ceiling:	8530m (28,000ft)
Maximum range:	around 930km (580 miles)
Armament:	four 20mm Hispano cannon in wings, plus underwing racks for up to 900kg (4000lb) of other weapons
First flight:	22 December 1941

The Fairey Firefly was a powerful two-seat fighter, designed for use by the Royal Navy onboard aircraft carriers. The short, broad wings were equipped with special flaps for low-speed flying, which could be recessed into the wing at higher speeds. The pilot was positioned over the leading edge of the wing and the observer was stationed behind it. The wings were folded manually for storage on the carrier. Later versions were used as night-fighters and for specialist anti-submarine operations. The final version was a three-seater aircraft. The Firefly saw active service in practically all theatres of engagement during the war. Altogether almost 2000 Fireflies of various marks were produced. It was a powerful aircraft and played a vital role in the war effort.

GLOSTER G-41 METEOR

Type:	single-seat fighter
Engines:	two Rolls-Royce turbojets; first service aircraft fitted with Rolls-Royce Welland
Wingspan:	13.1m (43ft)
Length:	12.6m (41ft 4in)
Height:	4m (13ft)
Weight:	3693kg (8140lb) empty 6260kg (13,800lb) loaded
Maximum speed:	660km/h (410 mph)
Service ceiling:	12,200-13,400m (40-44,000ft)
Maximum range:	1600km (1000 miles)
Armament:	four 20mm Hispano cannon at the side of the nose
First flight:	5 March 1943

The Gloster Meteor was the first jet combat aircraft to be designed by the Allies in the Second World War. The designer was George Carter. The early versions performed poorly, but improved engines developed by Rolls-Royce turned the Meteor into a high-performance aircraft that could deliver remarkable rates of acceleration and climb and sustained speeds. Sixteen Meteors entered service on 12 July 1944 with 616 Squadron. The first role assigned to the new aircraft was intercepting the V1 flying bombs that were being launched against Britain by the Germans. The Meteor was later developed as a reconnaissance aircraft, a jet trainer and a two-seat night fighter. In 1945 a Meteor set a new world speed record of 967km/h (606mph).

HAWKER HURRICANE

Type: single-seat fighter

Engines: Rolls-Royce Merlin v12, liquid-cooled

Wingspan: 12.2m (40ft)

Length: 9.75m (32ft)

Height: 4m (13ft 1in)

Weight: 2118kg (4670lb) empty, 2994kg (6600lb) loaded (Mark I)

Maximum speed: 511km/h (318mph) (Mark I)

Service ceiling: 11,000m (36,000ft) (Mark I)

Maximum range: 740km (460 miles)

Armament: eight 0.303 Brownings (Mark I), later versions equipped to carry bombs and rockets

First flight: prototype: 6 November 1935, Mark I: 12 October 1937

In June 1936 the new Hawker Hurricane was ordered in unprecedented numbers by the Air Ministry after the prototype passed its tests with flying colours. By September 1939, when war broke out, nearly 500 had been delivered to active squadrons and by the Battle of Britain, the following year, over 2300 were in service, making it the most numerous of the RAF's combat aircraft of the time. The Hurricane, powerfully equipped with eight machine-guns, proved to be a first-rate weapon against German bombers. For the North African campaign, they were equipped with tank-destroying 40mm cannon and a Sea Hurricane version, designed for launch by catapult from the decks of merchant ships, was also built. In all, over 14,000 Hurricanes were produced.

HAWKER TYPHOON

Type:	single-seat fighter-bomber
Engines:	2180hp Napier Sabre II, 24-cylinder, liquid-cooled
Wingspan:	12.7m (41ft 7in)
Length:	9.7m (31ft 11in)
Height:	4.7m (15ft 4in)
Weight:	3992kg (8800lb) empty, 6010kg (13,250lb) loaded
Maximum speed:	664 km/h (412mph)
Service ceiling:	10,730m (35,200ft)
Maximum range:	820km (510 miles), 1580km (980 miles) with drop tanks
Armament:	four 20mm Hispano cannon in wings, racks for eight rockets or two 227kg (500lb) bombs
First flight:	24 February 1940

The Hawker Typhoon had a troubled early development.
The first engine types tried out in the aircraft proved to be
unreliable, problems were encountered with the fuselage
and performance was disappointing. Additionally, work
was held up as most of the effort at the Hawker plants was
directed towards producing Hurricanes. However,
Typhoons began to be deployed to active squadrons in
September 1941, and the problems were gradually
overcome. By the end of 1942 the Typhoon was proving to
be effective against the Luftwaffe's fast fighter-bombers.
By 1944, hundreds of Typhoons, equipped with rockets
and bombs, were in round-the-clock action against
German ground forces in Europe, taking a heavy toll of
tanks and other equipment.

HAWKER TEMPEST

Type:	single-seat fighter-bomber
Engines:	2180hp Napier Sabre II 24-cylinder liquid-cooled
Wingspan:	12.5m (41ft)
Length:	10.25m (33ft 8in)
Height:	4.9m (16ft 1in)
Weight:	4128kg (9100lb empty), 6130kg (13,500lb) loaded
Maximum speed:	704 km/h (438mph) (Mark VI)
Service ceiling:	11,280m (37,000ft)
Maximum range:	1190km (740 miles)
Armament:	four Hispano cannon in outer wings, racks under wings for eight rockets or up to 900kg (2000lb) of bombs
First flight:	2 September 1942

The Hawker Tempest was one of the later combat aircraft to be developed in World War II. The Tempest came about as a result of a redesign of the earlier Hawker Typhoon, with, among other modifications, the wings altered to improve handling at high speeds. The Tempest was a faster aircraft than the Typhoon and was at the forefront of the RAF's efforts to protect targets in Britain from the German V1 'flying bombs'. In all, Tempests accounted for over a third of the flying bombs shot down by the RAF in 1944. It also proved itself invaluable in asserting air superiority for the Allies after the D-Day landings in June 1944. A version of the Tempest with a more powerful engine arrived too late to see combat, going into service in November 1945.

SUPERMARINE SPITFIRE

Type: single-seat fighter (statistics are for Mark IX)

Engines: Rolls-Royce Merlin 61, liquid-cooled

Wingspan: 11.2m (36ft 10in)

Length: 9.1m (29ft 11in)

Height: 3.5m (11ft 5in)

Weight: 2545kg (5610lb) empty, 4310kg (9500lb) loaded

Maximum speed: 657 km/h (408mph)

Service ceiling: 12,200m (40,000ft)

Maximum range: 700km (434 miles)

Armament: two 20mm Hispano cannon and four 0.303in Browning machine-guns in wings, centreline rack for drop tank or 227kg (500lb) bomb

First flight: 5 March 1936 (prototype)

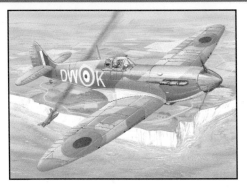

The Supermarine Spitfire, designed by Reginald Mitchell, is one of the most famous of all combat aircraft. Many different versions of this classic fighter were produced, among them the Seafire carrier-based fighter, some reconnaissance marks and fighter-bomber variants. The origins of the Spitfire began with a series of racing seaplanes designed by Mitchell in the 1920s. Flight tests of the Mark I Spitfire in 1936 exceeded all expectations and full-scale production began in 1937. By October 1939, well over 4000 aircraft had been ordered. Throughout the war, Mitchell continued to improve the Spitfire in an effort to keep ahead of its great rivals, the Messerschmitt Bf109 and FockeWulf Fw190. The Spitfire was so successful that it continued in service well into the 1950s.

WESTLAND WHIRLWIND

Type:	single-seat fighter (later fighter-bomber)
Engines:	two 885hp Rolls-Royce Peregrine I, liquid-cooled
Wingspan:	13.7m (45ft)
Length:	10m (32ft 9in)
Height:	3.5m (11ft 7in)
Weight:	3700kg (7840lb) empty, 4658kg (10,270lb) loaded
Maximum speed:	580km/h (360 mph)
Service ceiling:	9150m (30,000ft)
Maximum range:	1290km (800 miles)
Armament:	four 20mm Hispano MkI cannon in nose, underwing rack for 454kg (1000lb) bomb load added on Mark IA model
First flight:	11 October 1938

The twin-engined Westland Whirlwind was initially designed to provide long-range escort cover and carried formidable firepower in its nose guns. It was generally considered to be a fine aircraft to fly, but drawbacks such as trouble with the unreliable engine and its high landing speed of 130km/h (80mph) resulted in the Whirlwind being placed with only two squadrons. They acquitted themselves well in combat, escorting daylight bombing missions to Germany. Later they were equipped with bomb racks and these 'Whirlibombers' flew across the Channel on 'Rhubarb' sorties, attacking whichever targets presented themselves. Two hundred Whirlwinds were ordered but, because of the engine problems, many were cancelled and only 112 were built in all.

MACCHI C.202

Type:	single-seat fighter (some deployed as fighter-bombers
Engines:	1175hp Alfa Romeo RA1000 RC41-I
Wingspan:	10.6m (34ft 8in)
Length:	8.85m (29ft)
Height:	3m (12ft)
Weight:	2350kg (5181lb) empty, 3010kg (6636lb) loaded
Maximum speed:	595km/h (370mph)
Service ceiling:	11,000m (36,000ft)
Maximum range:	not available
Armament:	two 12.7mm Breda-SAFAT machine-guns above the engine, two 7.7mm Breda-SAFAT machine-guns in wings
First flight:	10 August 1940

The Macchi C.202 was developed from the earlier MC200 Saetta but was equipped with much more powerful engines than that aircraft. In terms of its armament it was somewhat under-equipped in comparison to the fighters of other air forces but its agility in flight meant it could outperform the Hawker Hurricane and the P40 Kittihawk, for example, in a dogfight and it was one of the best fighters of the Second World War. A few were equipped with underwing bomb racks and flew as fighter-bombers. The later 205 series was more formidably armed and handled just as well as the 202, but the Italian industries responsible for its production proved unequal to the task of producing them in any numbers.

REGGIÁNE RE 2000

Type:	single-seat fighter
Engines:	1025hp Piaggio P.XIbis RC40 radial
Wingspan:	11m (36ft 1in)
Length:	7.95m (26ft 3in)
Height:	3.15m (10ft 4in)
Weight:	1905kg (4200lb) empty, 2595kg (5722lb) loaded
Maximum speed:	535km/h (332mph)
Service ceiling:	11,200m (36,745 ft)
Maximum range:	950km (590 miles)
Armament:	two 12.7mm Breda-SAFAT machine guns, rack for 200kg (441lb) bomb; 2005 series additionally had three 20mm wing guns.
First flight:	1938 (2000 series), 1940 (2001 series), late 1941 (2002 series), September 1942 (2005 series)

The Reggiáne Re 2000 series were lightly built and highly manoeuvrable aircraft. Almost all of the first production of Re 2000s in fact served with the Swedish and Hungarian (as shown here) air forces, rather than with the Italian. A version of the Re 2000 was also tried out as a catapult-launched fighter for deployment on board Italian navy battleships. The 2001 series that followed was employed in both night fighter and day fighter roles by the Italian airforce, the Luftwaffe and with the Co-Belligerent Air Force, formed after the Italian surrender in 1943. The Re 2002 and 2005, although excellent aircraft, were only built in small numbers, with no more than 50 of each of the new marks seeing service before the end of the war.

KAWANISHI N1K2-J

Type: single-seat fighter

Engines: 1990hp Nakajima Homare 21 radial

Wingspan: 11.97m (39ft 3in)

Length: 8.89m (29ft 2in)

Height: 3.96m (13ft)

Weight: 2657kg (6299lb) empty, 4860kg (10,714lb) loaded

Maximum speed: 594km/h (369mph)

Service ceiling: 10,760m (35,400 ft)

Maximum range: 1720km (1069 miles)

Armament: four 20mm machine-guns in pairs inside wing, plus two 250kg (550lb) bombs on underwing racks, or six rockets mounted under the fuselage

First flight: 24 July 1943 (N1K1-J), 3 April 1944 (N1K2-J)

The Kawanishi N1K1-J Shiden, codenamed 'George' by the Allies, was potentially an outstanding fighter aircraft, despite some of the problems it faced. There were problems with the unreliable Nakajima Homare engine, which was almost impossible to service, and the landing gear was weak. This second fault arose from the fact that the aircraft had been developed from the N1K1 seaplane by among other things, removing the central float. The N1K2-J had an improved airframe and could be built quicky as it used far fewer parts, but was still plagued by engine problems. It was planned to build huge numbers of these aircraft but they failed to materialise. Both types were superbly manoeuvrable and highly respected by the Allied pilots who encountered them.

KAWASAKI Ki-61

Type:	single-seat fighter
Engines:	1175hp Kawasaki Ha-40; later 1450hp Ha-140; Ki-100 1500hp Mitsubishi Ha-11, liquid cooled
Wingspan:	12m (39ft 5in)
Length:	8.94m (29ft 4in)
Height:	3.7m (12ft 2in)
Weight:	2630kg (5798lb) empty, 3470kg (7650lb) loaded (Ki-61-I)
Maximum speed:	560km/h (348 mph) (Ki-61-I)
Service ceiling:	10,000m (32,800ft) (Ki-61-I)
Maximum range:	1800km (1100 miles) (Ki-61-I)
Armament:	two 20mm MG 150/20 in wings, two 7.7mm machine-guns above engine; Ki-100: two 20mm Ho-5 in wings and two 12.7mm in fuselage, plus racks for two 250kg (551lb) bombs
First flight:	December 1941, 1 February 1945 (Ki-100)

The Kawasaki Ki-61 Hien, codenamed 'Tony' were the only fighters in the Japanese air force to employ a liquid-cooled engine. This was based on a German designed engine, that was built under licence by Kawasaki. Over 2500 of these fighters were produced, first seeing action around New Guinea in 1943, and continuing to fly combat missions throughout the war. In 1945 a number of Ki-61 airframes were fitted with an improved engine. The resulting Ki-100 turned out to be one of the best fighters of the war and certainly the best the Japanese managed to produce. The Ki-100 units that were hastily sent into service proved to be formidable foes and caused heavy losses among Allied aircraft up to the end of the war.

MITSUBISHI A6M ZERO-SEN

Type:	single-seat carrier-based fighter (statistics are for A6M2)
Engines:	925hp Nakajima NK1C Sakae 12
Wingspan:	12m (39ft 5in)
Length:	9.06m (29ft 9in)
Height:	2.92m (9ft 7in)
Weight:	1680kg (3704lb) empty, 2410kg (5313lb) loaded
Maximum speed:	509km/h (316mph)
Service ceiling:	10,300m (33,790 ft)
Maximum range:	3110km (1940 miles) with drop tanks
Armament:	two 20mm Type 99 cannon with 60-round drums in outer wings, two 7.7mm Type 97 machine-guns above front fuselage, wing racks for two 30kg (66lb) bombs
First flight:	1 April 1939

The Mitsubishi A6M Zero-Sen, codenamed 'Zeke' is one of the best-known World War II combat aircraft. This superb carrier-based fighter was the principal attacker at Pearl Harbor in 1941 and appeared to take Allied planners completely by surprise. For the first few years of the war the Zeroes swept away all opposition, combining long-range endurance, excellent manoeuvrability and fearsome armament. It wasn't until the Grumman Hellcat and Corsair came into service with the US forces in 1943 that the Zero found itself up against a more formidable opponent. The final Zero model to be produced was the A6M7 Kamikaze version, intended for suicide attacks on Allied ships. In all almost 11,000 Zeroes were produced, fighting throughout the Pacific arena.

NAKAJIMA Ki-43 HAYABUSA

Type: single-seat interceptor fighter (statistics refer to Ki-43-I series)

Engines: 975hp Nakajima Ha-25 Sakae

Wingspan: 11.53m (37ft 10in)

Length: 8.82m (29ft)

Height: 3.27m (10ft 9in)

Weight: 1975kg (4354lb) empty, 2642kg (5824lb) loaded

Maximum speed: 493km/h (308mph)

Service ceiling: 11,850m (38,500 ft)

Maximum range: 1200km (750 miles)

Armament: two 7.7mm Type 80 machine-guns above engine, later versions of Mark I had one 7.7mm and one 12.7mm gun, then two 12.7mm guns

First flight: January 1939

The Nakajima Ki-43 Hayabusa, codenamed 'Oscar', was produced in numbers second only to those of the Zero-Sen and was the most numerous of Japan's land-based aircraft. As a dogfighter, the 'Oscar' was unsurpassed, outmanoeuvring any aircraft that came up against it, and it was very popular with its Army pilots. Its biggest drawback was that the aircraft was so cutdown for manoeuvrability that it was likely to disintegrate under fire. It was also lacking in firepower, but this deficiency was made up by the skill and accurate shooting of the men who flew it. Later versions were equipped with armour, affording some degree of protection. Almost 6000 of this fighter were produced and it saw action in every Japanese battle.

NAKAJIMA Ki-84 HAYATE

Type: single-seat fighter-bomber

Engines: 1900hp Nakajima Homare Ha-45

Wingspan: 11.24m (36ft 10in)

Length: 9.92m (32ft 6in)

Height: 3.39m (11ft 1in)

Weight: 2680kg (5864lb) empty, 3750kg (8267lb) loaded, 4150kg (9150lb) maximum overload

Maximum speed: 624km/h (388mph)

Service ceiling: 10,500m (34,450 ft)

Maximum range: 1650km (1025 miles), 2920km (1815

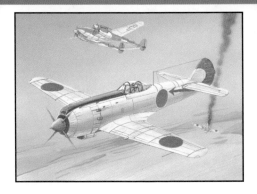

The Nakajima Ki-84 Hayate, codenamed 'Frank', was generally regarded as one of the Japanese Imperial Army's more formidable fighters. Its engine required a great deal of maintenance, but despite this was a powerful piece of equipment and gave the aircraft superb capabilities. Coming into service towards the end of the war, the Hayate was plagued by lack and quality of parts and often its pilots had no idea how their aircraft were going to perform. Despite the problems the Hayate was a superb aircraft and when flying at peak performance could outmanoeuvre most other aircraft. Over 3500 Hayates were produced in a variety of forms, often dictated by the availability of materials, with even a wooden prototype being designed.

ILYUSHIN IL-2 STORMOVIK

Type: single-seat or twin-seat close support
                       and attack

Engines: 1300hp M-38; after 1942 1750hp
                       AM38-F, liquid cooled

Wingspan: 14.6m (47ft 11in)

Length: 12m (39ft 4in)

Height: 3.4m (11ft 2in)

Weight: 3250kg (7165lb) empty, 5872kg
                       (12,947lb) loaded

Maximum speed: 450km/h (281mph), 370km/h (231mph)
                       with bomb load

Service ceiling: 6500m (21,300ft) with bomb load

Maximum range: 600km (373 miles) with bomb load

Armament: two 20mm ShVAK cannon and two
                       7.62mm ShKAS machine-guns in wing,
                       racks for eight 82mm rockets and four
                       bombs

First flight: March 1941

The Ilyushin Il-2 Stormovik had the biggest production run of any aircraft in World War II and, with all versions taken into account, more than 42,000 were produced. The Stormovik was armoured with steel and later versions were equipped with powerful engines. The single-seat version was heavily armed and equipped with ground-attack rockets. The two-seat version was even more formidable, with a rear gun and heavy anti-tank armament. The Stormovik played a decisive role along the Eastern Front, not only taking on the Luftwaffe's Me109s, but also successfully engaging and destroying Tiger and Panther tanks on the ground, with pairs of aircraft not uncommonly making devastating attack runs just above ground level.

MIKOYAN-GUREVICH MiG-3

Type:	single-seat fighter
Engines:	1350hp AM-35A
Wingspan:	10.3m (33ft 9in)
Length:	8.15m (26ft 9in)
Height:	2.61m (8ft 7in)
Weight:	weight empty is unknown, loaded weight probably around 3490kg (7695lb)
Maximum speed:	640km/h (398mph)
Service ceiling:	12,000m (39,370ft)
Maximum range:	1250km (780 miles)
Armament:	one 12.7mm BS and two 7.62mm ShKAS machine-guns in nose, two more BSs added in underwing pods later, plus rails for six RS-82 rockets
First flight:	around May 1941

The Mikoyan-Gurevich MiG-3 was one of the first of a long line of combat aircraft that continues to the present day, designed by the partnership of Mikoyan and Gurevich. The MiG-1, made of metal and wood was an average performer with a tendency to swing alarmingly on take-off and landing. However, it was designed and produced with great speed and over 2000 went into service. The MiG-3 had a more powerful engine and a greater range. It was also better armed than its predecessor. However, it proved to be totally out-matched by the Luftwaffe fighters it encountered and was soon withdrawn from regular combat duties. Instead, it was employed in close support and reconnaissance roles.

POLIKARPOV I-16

Type: single-seat fighter

Engines: 480hp M-22 in Type 1, later types had 725hp, 775hp, 1000hp engines

Wingspan: 9m (29ft 7in)

Length: 6.08m (19ft 11in)

Height: 2.45m (8ft 1in)

Weight: Type 1: 998kg (2200lb) empty, 1345kg (2965lb) loaded

Maximum speed: Type 1: 360km/h (224mph), Type 24: 525km/h (326mph)

Service ceiling: 9000m (29,500ft)

Maximum range: 800km (500 miles)

Armament: Type 1: two 7.62mm ShKAS machine-guns in wings, later versions had two 20mm ShVAK cannon in wings, two ShKAS in fuselage, many fitted with rails for two rockets

First flight: 31 December 1933

The Polikarpov I-16 was a remarkable aircraft. This short and stubby little fighter was, when it first went into production in 1933, capable of a surprising turn of speed and was around 110km/h (70mph) faster than other fighters. It first saw combat in the Spanish Civil War on the Republican side, where it performed well, causing havoc with its fast climbing and diving and overall manoeuvrability. Against the Luftwaffe's Messerschmitt Bf109s the I-16 found itself outclassed but, despite heavy losses the Soviet fighters continued to take on their enemy. Some were even specially modified for use in ramming attacks against the German planes. Later versions were modified as dive bombers and as two-seat training aircraft.

YAKOVLEV YAK-1

Type: single-seat fighter

Engines: 1100hp VK-105PA, liquid-cooled; later 1260hp VK-105PF

Wingspan: 10m (32ft 10in)

Length: 8.48m (27ft 10in)

Height: 2.64m (8ft 8in)

Weight: 2375kg (5137lb) empty, 2890kg (6217lb) loaded

Maximum speed: 600km/h (373mph)

Service ceiling: 10,000m (32,800ft)

Maximum range: 850km (580 miles)

Armament: one 20mm ShVAK cannon firing through propeller, one or two 12.7mm Beresin BS machine-guns above engine, underwing rails for six 12kg (25lb) RS-82 rockets

First flight: March 1939

The Yakovlev Yak-1 was given the go ahead to begin production in the same month, June 1941, that Germany invaded the Soviet Union. With a delay of only six weeks in the delivery schedule, the production line was dismantled and moved 1000 miles eastward out of reach of the invaders. This was the beginning of one of the biggest of all production programmes, with around 37,000 fighters being delivered by the end of the war. With its wooden wings and steel body, the Yak-1 was an agile flier, handling well in the air and, just as importantly, it was easy to maintain and reliable. Later modifications to improve the view from the rear of the cockpit by modifying the fuselage led to the aircraft's redesignation as the Yak-7.

CURTISS P-40 HAWK

Type: single-seat fighter, reconnaissance, ground attack and fighter-bomber (statistics are for P-40F Kittihawk)

Engines: 1300hp Packard V-1650-1

Wingspan: 11.36m (37ft 4in)

Length: 9.55m (31ft 2in)

Height: 3.75m (12ft 4in)

Weight: 2974kg (6550lb) empty, 3960kg (8720lb) loaded

Maximum speed: 680km/h (364mph)

Service ceiling: 9150m (30,000 ft)

Maximum range: 980km (610 miles)

Armament: six 0.5in Browning machine-guns in wings, one 226kg (500lb) bomb on centre rack and one 113kg (250lb) bomb under each wing

First flight: Model 75 prototype May 1935, P-40 January 1940

The first of the various versions of the Curtiss Hawk, the Hawk P75A, began its wartime career in the service of the French air force, giving a first-class account of itself against the Luftwaffe, even though completely outnumbered. Improvements, involving a new liquid-cooled engine, took a long time, but by the end of 1940 the first P-40s were combat ready. These were strong machines and highly manoeuvrable, although no match for the best fighters of the Luftwaffe, such as the Messerschmitt Bf109. However, if it was no dogfighter, the Hawk still had a strong role to play in providing support for ground troops. It saw service with the air forces of over twenty countries, the United States alone taking delivery of almost 14,000.

GRUMMAN F4F WILDCAT

Type:	single-seat naval fighter (statistics are for F4F-4)
Engines:	one 1200hp Pratt & Whitney R-1830-86
Wingspan:	11.6m (38ft)
Length:	8.5m (28ft 10in)
Height:	3.6m (11ft 11in)
Weight:	2110kg (4649lb) empty, 2770kg (6100lb), later 3600kg (7950lb), loaded
Maximum speed:	509km/h (318mph)
Service ceiling:	10,670m (35,000ft)
Maximum range:	1450km (900 miles)
Armament:	six 0.5in Colt-Browning machine-guns in outer wings, two 113kg (250lb) bombs carried in underwing racks
First flight:	2 September 1937

The aircraft that eventually became the Grumman F4F Wildcat was originally planned to be a biplane, but was redesigned as a monoplane before it went into production. The first batch of XF4F-3s, named the Martlet I, found their way into service with the Britiish Fleet Air Arm in 1939. As production gathered pace, improvements were made, including fitting folding wings on the F4F-4, and the aircraft was renamed the Wildcat. Thousands came into service with the US Navy and Marines. In hundreds of combat actions in both the European and Pacific theatres of war, this tough little aircraft, able to operate off small carrier decks, lived up to its name. The heavyweight F4F-7 was a reconnaissance plane that could stay airborne for close to 24 hours.

GRUMMAN F6F HELLCAT

Type: single-seat naval fighter

Engines: 2000hp Pratt & Whitney R2800-10; later 2200hp Pratt & Whitney R2800-10W

Wingspan: 13.05m (42ft 10in)

Length: 10.2m (33ft 7in)

Height: 4m (13ft 1in)

Weight: F6F-3 4101kg (9042lb) empty, 5528kg (12186lb) loaded

Maximum speed: F6F-3 605km/h (376mph)

Service ceiling: 11,430m (37,500ft)

Maximum range: 1755km (1090 miles) on internal fuel tanks

Armament: six 0.5in Browning machine-guns in outer wings, some marks had under wing attachments for six rockets and pylons for bombs

First flight: 26 June 1942

The Grumman F6F Hellcat was one of the classic aircraft of the Second World War. Developed from the F4F Wildcat, the Hellcat was soon coming off the production line in great numbers at the beginning of 1943. By the end of the war, over 12,000 of these tough aircraft were delivered. The Hellcat made a telling difference to the campaign in the Pacific right from its first combat appearance. Although not particularly fast, it completely out-matched anything the Japanese could put in the air against it in terms of strength and firepower. A number of Hellcats also fought in Europe with the British Fleet Air Arm. Later versions of the Hellcat were equipped as night fighters and for photographic reconnaissance duties.

LOCKHEED P-38 LIGHTNING

Type: single-seat long-range fighter (statistics are for P-38G)

Engines: two 1325hp Allison V-1710, liquid-cooled

Wingspan: 15.86m (52ft)

Length: 11.53m (37ft 10in)

Height: 3.9m (12ft 10in)

Weight: around 5770kg (12,700lb) empty, 8980kg (19,800lb) loaded

Maximum speed: 630-66km/h (391-414mph)

Service ceiling: 12,190m (40,000ft)

Maximum range: 3650km (2260 miles) with maximum fuel

Armament: one 37mm Oldsmobile cannon, four 0.5in Browning machine-guns, inner-wing pylons for 452kg (1000lb) bombs

First flight: 27 January 1939

The Lockheed P-38 Lightning came about in answer to the United States' requirement for a long-range pursuit fighter and escort. Although it ran into problems on its first test outings, the US Air Corps were very impressed by the twin-hulled Lightning's endurance and gave Lockheed the go-ahead to continue its development. Their confidence in the new aircraft was not misplaced. Within minutes of the USA declaring war in December 1941, a Lightning had recorded its first victory, shooting down a German bomber off Iceland. In the course of the war P-38s were in action over the North Atlantic, the Pacific and in Africa. In total, almost 10,000 Lightnings went into service, including a version capable of carrying 1800kg (4000lb) of bombs.

NORTH AMERICAN P-51 MUSTANG

Type: single-seat fighter, also attack bomber
                       and reconnaissance versions (statistics
                       are for the P-51D)

Engines: 1520hp Packard V-1650-3

Wingspan: 11.29m (37ft)

Length: 9.81m (32ft 3in)

Height: 4.1m (13ft 8in)

Weight: 3230kg (7125lb) empty, 5206kg
                       (11,600lb) loaded

Maximum speed: 703km/h (437mph)

Service ceiling: 12,770m (41,900ft)

Maximum range: with drop tanks 3200km (2000 miles),
                   combat range 1520km (950 miles)

Armament: six 0.5in Browning MG53-2 machine-
                       guns and wing racks for two 454kg
                       (1000lb) bombs or drop tanks

First flight: 26 October 1940

The North American P-51 Mustang was originally
commissioned from North American Aviation by the
British Air Purchasing Commission in 1940. Designed,
built and flown in an incredibly short time, it was so
impressive that it was soon being placed with US Army
squadrons as well as with the RAF. The Mustang was
capable of supplying long-distance escort protection for
bombers flying missions all the way to Berlin and back
from their bases in Britain. Fitted with drop tanks they
were able to fly 3200-km (2000-mile) round trips. During
the course of the war over 15,500 of these excellent
aircraft were produced. Such was its success that, after
the war, over 50 countries adopted the Mustang in their
air forces.

NORTHROP P-61 BLACK WIDOW

Type: three-seat night fighter

Engines: two 2000hp Pratt & Whitney R-2800 Double Wasp radials

Wingspan: 20.12m (66ft)

Length: 15.1m (49ft 7in)

Height: 4.49m (14ft 8in)

Weight: 10,886kg (24,000 lb) empty, 17,237kg (38,000 lb) loaded (P-61B)

Maximum speed: 692km/h (430mph) (P-61D)

Service ceiling: 12,500m (41,000ft) (P-61D)

Maximum range: 4500km (2800 miles) with maximum fuel

Armament: four 20mm M2 cannon in belly, plus electric dorsal turret in some versions, fired by pilot, underwing racks for bombs in later versions

First flight: 21 May 1942

The Northrop Black Widow was the first aircraft to be designed from the outset as a night-fighter. It was a large aircraft as it had to accommodate not only the pilot and gunner, but also the operator in charge of the latest radar technology with which the aircraft was equipped. Although big, the Black Widow was highly manoeuvrable. The name came from the all-black colour scheme, designed to reduce visibility. Original versions were fitted with a gun turret, positioned well to the rear of the cockpit, but this caused instabilities in flight when it was fired and was dropped from later models. First flown in the Pacific Theatre, the Black Widow soon showed its worth in Europe as well. Less than a thousand of this advanced aircraft were built during the war.

REPUBLIC P-47 THUNDERBOLT

Type: single-seat fighter, later fighter-bomber

Engines: 2000hp Pratt & Whitney R-2800
Double Wasp radial

Wingspan: 12.4m (40ft 9in)

Length: 11.03m (36ft 1in)

Height: 4.3m (14ft 2in)

Weight: 4853kg (10,700lb) empty, 8800kg
(19,400lb) loaded (P-47D)

Maximum speed: 690km/h (428mph) (P-47D)

Service ceiling: 13,000m (42,000ft)

Maximum range: 1600km (1000 miles), 3060km (1900
miles) with drop tanks (P-47D)

Armament: eight 0.5in Colt-Browning M-2
machine-guns in wings, three to five
wing racks for bombs and rockets or
fuel tanks

First flight: 6 May 1941

The Republic P-47 Thunderbolt was soon christened the 'Jug', on account of its juggernaut proportions. Designed around a new engine, it had to be made big to accommodate it. A number of technical difficulties were overcome and the P-47 went into production in 1942. All the painstaking problem-solving was worthwhile. The 'Jug' went into service at the beginning of 1943 with the US 8th Air Force in Britain and proved itself a tough fighter – one fighter group recording the biggest number of kills of any in the Second World War. In all, 15,660 Thunderbolts were produced and they made a telling impact on the enemy in both the Pacific and European theatres of war. It was also capable of carrying a considerable bomb load deep into enemy territory.

VOUGHT V-166 CORSAIR

Type: single-seat carrier-based fighter-bomber
                     (also reconnaissance and night-fighter)

Engines: 2450hp Pratt & Whitney R-2800
                     Double Wasp radial

Wingspan: 12.5m (41ft)

Length: 10.3m (33ft 8in)

Height: 4.5m (16ft 1in)

Weight: 4025kg (8873lb) empty, 6350kg
                     (14,000lb) loaded

Maximum speed: 635km/h (395mph)

Service ceiling: 11,280m (37,000ft)

Maximum range: 1600km (1000 miles) on internal tanks

Armament: four 20mm cannon or six 0.5in
                     Browning machine-guns, later versions
                     equipped with racks for two 450kg
                     (1000lb) bombs or six rockets

First flight: 29 May 1940

The Vought Corsair was one of the Second World War's greatest aircraft. It enjoyed the longest production run of any US aircraft of the time, from 1942 to 1952, when the last of the 12,571 Corsairs rolled out of the factory. The prototype was fitted with the most powerful engine available at the time and was the first US combat aircraft to exceed 640km/h (400mph) and soon proved itself able to outperform all other US fighters. First going into action in the Solomon Islands in the Pacific in 1943, it quickly proved that it could outperform the Japanese fighters it encountered as well, taking out 11 enemy aircraft for every loss incurred. Later variants were equipped for reconnaissance, night-fighter and fighter-bomber roles with considerable success.

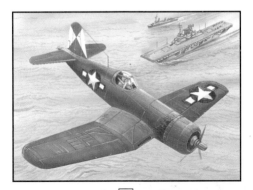

The Battle of Britain

On 5 June 1940 the first Luftwaffe bombers appeared over Britain. This was the beginning of a battle that was to prove decisive in determining the outcome of the war in Europe – the Battle of Britain had begun.

If the German Army was to have any chance of invading Britain successfully then it was vital that the Luftwaffe first gain control of the air. The Germans had nearly 3000 aircraft available for the attack, against them stood just 900 RAF fighters.

On Eagle Day, 13 August 1940, the German assault began. Over the course of the next ten days the skies over

Britain were criss-crossed by the contrails of dog-fighting aircraft. The Luftwaffe fighters were engaging the RAF at the limit of their range and this gave the British pilots an advantage. Losses on the German side mounted.

Then the Germans changed their tactics and began to concentrate their efforts against RAF Fighter Command's airfields. By the beginning of September the Germans had the upper hand as the RAF reeled under the losses of both airfields and aircrew.

On 7 September the Germans made a vital miscalculation. Believing that they had defeated the RAF they switched their assault to London. Relieved from the constant bombardment the RAF regrouped and on 15 September delivered a telling blow against the German bombers, shooting down 60 for the loss of only 26 fighters. As summer shaded into autumn and the weather began to deteriorate Hitler decided that the invasion of Britain would have to be postponed. Later he would call it off altogether. By the end of September the RAF had shot down 1099 German aircraft for the loss of 678 fighters. The Battle of Britain had been won and the course of the war altered decisively in the Allies' favour.

The War in the Pacific

Given the vast distances involved in this theatre it was inevitable that aircraft would play a vital role. On Sunday, 7 December 1941, over 360 aircraft from the Japanese carrier fleet launched an all-out assault on the American naval base at Pearl Harbor in the Hawaiian Islands, sinking or damaging many American ships but failing to destroy their aircraft carriers or fuel supplies.

Within six months the American aircrews had delivered devastating counter-strikes at the battles of the Coral Sea and Midway. These were battles in which the attacks were delivered entirely by air with no exchange of fire between ships.

By 1944, at the Battle of Leyte Gulf in the Philippines the Americans were able to put over 1000 planes into the air against just over 100 Japanese aircraft. Inevitably, Japan suffered a crushing defeat and their navy was effectively eliminated. The war in the Pacific was entering its final stages.

ANATOMY OF A FIGHTER PLANE

Navigation light

Bullet-proof windscreen

Constant speed propeller

Exhaust pipes

Carburettor air intake

.303in Brownings

20mm Hispano cannon

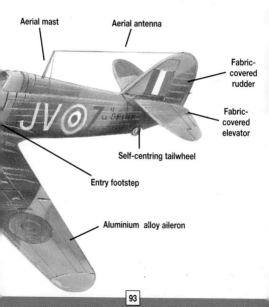

Aerial mast

Aerial antenna

Fabric-covered rudder

Fabric-covered elevator

Self-centring tailwheel

Entry footstep

Aluminium alloy aileron

93